It's Not About Me!

Step into the Fold

By
Kendall Belvedere Helmly

ISBN

Paperback: 978-1-965560-47-1

Hardcover: 978-1-965560-46-4

Moe walked on the
earth about 10,000
years ago.

※   ※   ※

Moe had long, shaggy
hair and a hump of
fat on his back to
help keep him warm.

❄   ❄   ❄

Moe had a long trunk, like an elephant, to help him smell and pick up food.

Moe used his long,
curved tusks to dig
for food in
the snow.

Woolly mammoths and elephants are related.

❄ ❄ ❄

Moe was bigger than
an elephant.

※   ※   ※

Moe lived in cold places of the world, like Russia, Alaska, Canada, and the USA.

Moe had four
legs and big,
floppy ears.

❄ ❄ ❄

Moe ate plants,
like grasses
and shrubs.

Some of Moe's
friends had long
beards and
mustaches.

※   ※   ※

Moe was very good
at surviving in
cold weather.

The babies of
mammoths were
called calves.

Moe and other woolly
mammoths lived in
herds and worked
together to
find food.

They used their
tusks to defend
themselves from
predators.

Scientists have
found frozen
mammoths in the
permafrost of
Siberia, Russia.

Scientists study the
fossil bones of
mammoths to learn
about how
they lived.

Moe and other
woolly mammoths are
now extinct and
no longer
live on earth.

Some scientists are
working to bring
mammoths back to
life, using a
process called
de-extinction.

Although wooly
mammoths are no
longer with us,
their legacy
lives on!

THE END

Find More books by Jenny Schreiber

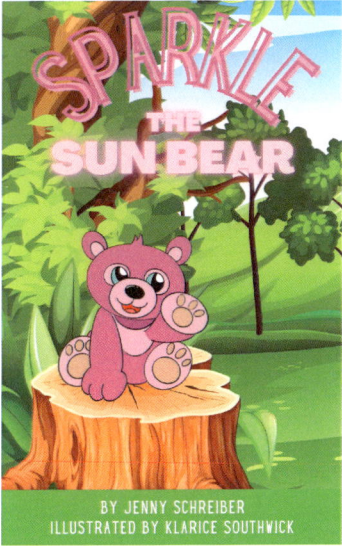

Sparkle the Sun Bear

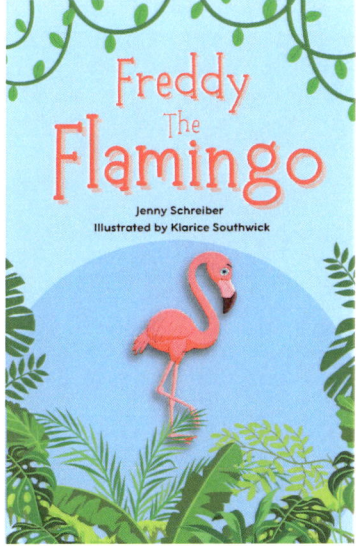

Freddy the Flamingo

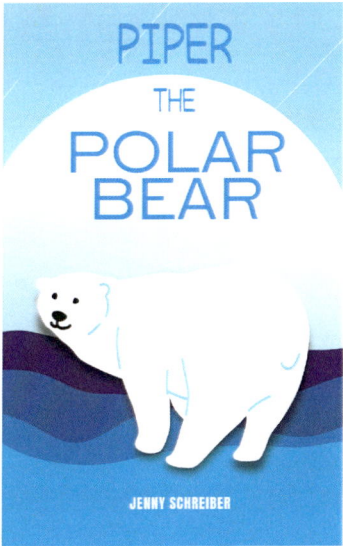

Piper the
Polar Bear

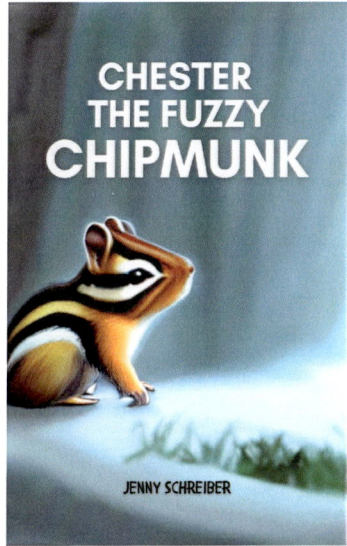

Chester the
Fuzzy Chipmunk

Animal Facts Children's Book Series

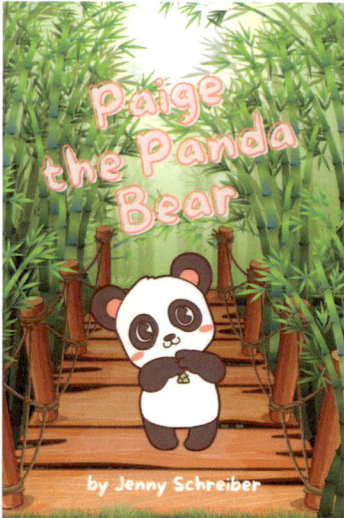

Paige the
Panda Bear

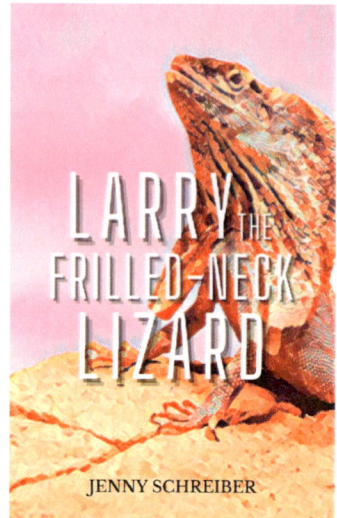

Larry the
Frilled-Neck Lizard

www.ingramcontent.com/pod-product-compliance
Lightning Source LLC
Chambersburg PA
CBRC101142030426
42335CB00007B/203